COMMUNICATE WAY MORE BETTER!

Scotty Gunther

www.coworkerschallenge.com

This book is dedicated to anyone who wants to talk good...and stuff.

Introduction

Communication is an important part of any business or work situation. Learning to be an effective communicator is a valuable skill, and one that is commonly overlooked. The effects of poor business communication can be truly destructive and result in hurt feelings, (crying) wasted time, misunderstandings, fights, disastrous meetings, unproductive teamwork, and lack of completion of common workplace goals!

This book is a fun, "tongue-in-cheek" look at proper communication in business through ten insightful tips and a collection of original quotes. It's the perfect accompaniment to my live motivational speeches, keynote address, or business seminars.

My goal was to write a simple, fun, easy to understand book about business communication that lightens the mood, makes you laugh, and helps you communicate WAY more better!

Tip: 1

Speak loud enough so others can hear you.

I don't have a problem with this, (I was born without an inside voice) but for some shy people, speaking up or projecting can be an issue. A commanding properly projected voice will make you appear to be a strong leader. Remember, in order for people to understand you, they will need to be able to...HEAR YOU! It's no different than if I decide to type in a font so small that it would be difficult for you to read this book. What's the point? You wouldn't be able to understand what I am trying to communicate. The first key to communicating better is communicating in a way that is easy for someone to understand!

Leadership...even the word leadership is interesting! Leader, which means to lead....and ship, which means...boat!? ~Scotty Gunther

You also need to speak in a clear "easy to understand" way.

I met a girl in Pittsburgh, who had a tongue ring. I asked her what she was studying in college and she answered cacmoonnacaton! Look, if you can't say it, you can't study it! ~Scotty Gunther

It's important to use the right words.

When my niece was really young, she was super smart...but she would sometimes get her words mixed up. One day she poked herself in the eye, and she was running around the house yelling..."I THINK I DAMAGED MY UTERUS! ~Scotty Gunther

I wanted another iced-tea, so I went through the fast food restaurant drive-thru for the third time that day. I apologized to the girl because she had to see me again, and she said, "NO, I like when you come through. You are funny, smart and sexy...you're like MY DAD!" ~Scotty Gunther

Know what you are talking about.

I asked the women, "how was dinner?" She answered "Well, the pork was dry and it tasted funny!" It was TURKEY! ~Scotty Gunther

She was telling me that her marriage isn't working because her husband won't communicate with her anymore. But when he does, he is mentally abusive and calls her "stupid" and an "idiot," all the time! I asked, "do you suspect infidelity?" She answered, "ABSOLUTELY NOT... but I think he might be cheating on me!" ~Scotty Gunther

Tip: 2

Learn to speak the other person's language.

Have you ever been talking to someone and even though you feel like you are communicating in a clear "easy to understand" way, the other person ends up just staring at you in a lost and confused way? How can they not understand what you are saying? Well, this is because even though you are communicating in your language, you are NOT speaking in THEIR language.

I walked into a fast-food restaurant in Texas and I ordered a salad. The woman asked, "Do you want lettuce on that?" ~Scotty Gunther

We all communicate in a way that we find comfortable to ourselves. But unless you are only talking to yourself, (which I do all the time) you might not speaking in the other person's language. Most communication issues happen because of misunderstandings, because one person is not speaking in the other person's language.

I was supposed to get married but it didn't work out. All of the problems surfaced when we started planning the wedding. We just wanted different things. I wanted a small intimate wedding. And SHE wanted...my friend Todd! ~Scotty Gunther

Remember that different generations communicate in different languages.

I told a woman that I was over 40 and then I said, "Age is only a number!" She answered, "Your age isn't a number, it's actually three letters...O...L...D!" ~Scotty Gunther!

Everyone gets older. It's a fact of life. I had a woman say to me, "Your gray hair make you look old. You should really do something about it." So I did...I bought a Cadillac! ~Scotty Gunther

So, what is speaking someone's language and how do you do it? Speaking in the other person's language is simply being aware that NOT

everyone will understand what you are saying!
Now, that's pretty simple. Try not to get frustrated
if they don't seem to get you or what you are
saying. Getting frustrated or mad at them will
only cause more of a disconnect.

Tip: 3

Be aware of nonverbal communication, whatever that means?

Most of our communication with anyone isn't just what we say but *how we say it*. I am "a yeller" and I use a lot of body language to communicate.

The doctor wanted to give me Ritalin to calm me down...but I ran away! ~Scotty Gunther

I come from a family of "yellers" and the only way to be heard was to yell over the other family members who were also yelling! Even though we were all yelling, it didn't mean that we were fighting. This is just how we communicated! To this very day, this still causes me problems. Even though I am not mad or angry, eight out of ten people I am communicating with will think I am excited, mad, or upset even when I am not! Observers who are not directly involved in the conversation often think that I am fighting with someone...when I am NOT. (I AM NOT FIGHTING! WANNA FIGHT ABOUT IT?)

Somebody asked me if I had ADHD. I answered, "I don't even have basic cable!" ~Scotty Gunther

What is nonverbal communication?

I asked him if he knew any nonverbal communication...and he said "YES," then he flipped me off! ~Scotty Gunther

Even if you are not aware of it, volume, tone and body language is just as important as -*what you are saying*. This is called nonverbal communication and while flipping the middle finger to someone who just cut you off in your car IS considered nonverbal communication, it's also much more!

Nonverbal communication? Do you mean like text messages?

So she said "I just got a text message from a friend. What does IDK stand for?" I answered "I don't know." And she replied, "NOBODY DOES!" ~Scotty Gunther

Nonverbal communication is your body language, the tone of your voice, inflection, eye contact, and even clothing and image.

You know it's time for a fashion makeover, when you go to 80's party in your own clothes and someone says, " I love your outfit!" ~Scotty Gunther

Being aware of "Body language" is more than just staring at someone's body.

I had a guy say "you are right about THIS body language thing. It really works. Because sometimes my mind is telling me no, but my body, my body is telling me...yes!" Thanks R Kelly. ~Scotty Gunther

I knew a guy whose body was out of shape so he wanted to take steroids. He couldn't get his hands on regular steroids but he worked at the zoo so he took monkey steroids. He got a little bigger but he kept having the urge to throw his poop at people. ~Scotty Gunther

Studies show that 93% of communication is non-verbal. Studies also show that 98% of all studies are statistically inaccurate.

Learning to communicate way more better means that you will need to learn how to read nonverbal signals as well as hearing what the other person is saying. Reading these nonverbal signals takes time and patience but the more you do it, the more attuned you will be to what they're really saying, such as:

- Folded arms in front of a person may mean they're feeling defensive or closed off. Or they could have sweaty armpits! (And if they are clinching their fists, it's time to run away!)

- Lack of eye contact may mean they're not really interested in what you're saying, are ashamed of something, or find it difficult to talk about something. (Or you just could be ugly.) If they just walk away while you are talking, that could also mean that they are not really interested in what you are saying.

- A louder more aggressive tone may mean the person is escalating the discussion and is becoming very emotionally involved. It might also suggest they feel like they're not being heard or understood. (Or maybe you are just talking to Scotty? He's a yeller!)

- Someone who's turned away from you when talking to you may mean disinterest or being closed off. (Or you might have funky bad breath.)

- If they are flipping you the middle finger... well, you KNOW what that means!

All the while you're reading someone's nonverbal signals, be aware of your own. Make and maintain eye contact, (without licking your lips) and keep a neutral body stance and tone to your voice. This way they won't feel like they are being yelled at.

Tip: 4

Learn to be less serious. Or you could DIE!

One of the main challenges we are all facing in the last decade or so, is the important fact that the whole world went out and got "all serious." Political correctness and super sensitive people have made it very difficult to communicate, because everybody is offended by everything! And EVERYBODY is now considered a bully! The dictionary's definition of "bully" is anyone who uses their power or position to intimidate someone else. So everybody who is your boss is a bully? This is crazy because there has always a pecking order in business. There is a pretty good chance that your boss started out in the mail room and was so called "bullied" by everyone in the building at one time.   It's NOT bullying, it's just called business! Keep in mind that I am NOT talking about sexual harassment. This is serious and should be reported immediately. What I am talking about is the simple fact that NOT everyone is going to say something that you like. People will hurt your feelings or communicate in a way that might offend you...but who cares? Get over it! Is what they are saying even true? Or is it just their opinion? If it's not true, it shouldn't offend you and if it IS true and you are ashamed of it...change it! This is why you need to learn how to be less serious, because humor and playfulness will help you rise above anything that might offend you.

I always eat a whole raw onion before I go to the dentist because I figure if he is going to make me cry, I might as well make him cry too! ~Scotty Gunther

You don't have to be funny in order to use humor and playfulness in everyday conversations. You just need to use the sense of humor you do have and try and inject it into more of your speaking and learn to lighten up. This is where a great sense of humor will help you tremendously. A great sense of humor helps lighten everyday frustrations and helps put things into perspective more gently than other methods.

Life is only as hard as you THINK it is. ~Scotty Gunther

Tip: 5

Appear to be open and honest.

There seems to be a recent trend where people say, "always be open and honest." Just tell the truth and everything will work out. In theory "open and honest" seems like a good idea. The truth is, IT NEVER WORKS! I am not telling you to be dishonest, but always telling the truth about what you think and feel can get you into trouble! Now, I know this might sound dishonest and you might start questioning my values and integrity. The problem with always being honest and open is, the people around you are NOT honest. It would be great if we lived in a perfect world where people weren't manipulative and not always out for themselves...BUT THEY ARE! If you are always open and honest, people will use this to destroy you. You may think always being honest is a good thing but pointing what is wrong, whose fault it is, giving unsolicited options, and never holding back judgment will eventually alienate EVERYONE around you! You will end up being the odd man or woman out. Terms like; Jerk, loudmouth, know it all, and _____hole will be used to describe you by co-workers! Now, I understand that this really doesn't matter to some individuals. In fact some people, (myself included) get a kick out of, (or actually define themselves by) stirring the pot!   If you are looking for long term employment, "always being honest" is not something that will help you reach your goal. Unless your goal is to be hated, unemployed and alone.

My mom said, "not everyone is going to like you"...BOY, WAS SHE RIGHT! ~Scotty Gunther

So what can you do? This might seem dishonest but if you would like to have friends and a job you will just have to "appear to be open and honest." Think about Hollywood stars. Based on their public persona, some seem very nice. But you don't truly know them. In fact, some of the people who seem the most down to earth are the biggest self-absorbed jerks on the planet. They "appear to be open and honest," and so should you. I am NOT saying that you need to be phony but telling you that being open and honest at all times is the best way to communicate is NOT being honest with you. Another great quick tip is; only get involved in business that is actually YOUR BUSINESS! You will find that this is actually a very small amount, so you have lots of time to spend working on your job! Which in turn will help you increase your value.

The only way you can tell your boss exactly what you think and feel...is IF... you are self-employed.. ~Scotty Gunther

Tip: 6

Avoid mimicking or mirroring others.

You might not be familiar with the terms mimicking or mirroring. The basic concept of mimicking or mirroring is simple. When interacting with another person, we should copy, or "mirror," some of that person's movements, facial expressions or words. We should adopt the other person's characteristics.

While some experts say mimicking or mirroring people creates a powerful sense of familiarity, comfort and trust, I find the whole concept odd. While it might occur naturally to some, I find copying the actions or movement of a person on purpose is just creepy and will make them self-conscious and uncomfortable.

If someone I am meeting with scratches their nose, I should scratch MY nose because that will make them more comfortable? NO, I don't scratch mine to mirror them. Because they told me subconsciously by their movement that I have something on MY nose. So I rub my nose, then they think something is wrong with their nose, so they rub their nose. And so on, and so on. I sure hope they don't rub their butt! It's hard to know who's truly copying whom?

Guys mature slower than women, it's just a fact. I was a late bloomer. I wet the bed until I was 12, which was a problem because I shared a bed with my brother. He thought he wet the bed until he was 16. ~Scotty Gunther

Tip: 7

Care about your customers and co-workers! (Or at least act like you do.)

When it comes to great customer service, communicating properly is very important! Good customer service is the key to any successful business. So you need to learn how to care about your customers or at least act like you do. Does that sound dishonest to you? It's NOT. Even if you are not a "people person" you need to realize that customers bring in the most important thing to growing your business and success. MONEY! Say it with me now. MONEY, MONEY, MONEY! Even if you are doing what you do, out of pure love of the craft, money will give you the opportunity to do it longer and better. And who has the money?

Customers have the money! So it's important to care about them. Even when they are wrong and crazy.

Crazy people don't know they are crazy!
~Scotty Gunther

You can offer great products, promotions and prices to bring in as many new customers, but unless you can get some of those customers to come back, your business won't be profitable for long. If you are in business, then ultimately customers matter.

We just want to be happy! Some people find happiness in the little things in life, while others find happiness by being unhappy all the time. They're called...customers. ~Scotty Gunther

The customer is NOT always right...but that's just too bad!

I am thinking about changing my name to drama...then, customers will LOVE me! ~Scotty Gunther

Being mean or disrespectful to your co-workers is NEVER a good idea. (Even if they ARE all morons!) I know this first hand because in the past, I have treated co-workers like they don't matter. I was raised to be independent and do everything yourself. When you are so much better than others, you can't expect the same out them as you would expect from yourself. I always thought I would just "do my own thing" but this is a quick way to alienate your co-workers.

Tip: 8

Become comfortable communicating in your own style!

Good communication skills require a high level of self-awareness. In order to communicate way more better, you will need to become comfortable with how you communicate. Becoming comfortable with your own style will go a long way toward helping you to create good and lasting impressions on others.

I am peanut butter pie! Have you ever had peanut butter pie? It might be the best food you have tasted. But, if you ate it every meal, it would make you sick! I am peanut butter pie!~Scotty Gunther

Because this is NOT a psychology book, I am not going to get into "what the basic communicating styles are" or "what they mean." I am going to just say, if what you are doing seems to work, then do more of that. And if it doesn't work, do something else. I know this seems wasteful and wishy-washy but the only true way of communicating way more better is to...communicate way more!

If you were born without an inside voice, try NOT to get a job in a library. But sometimes you are going to have to take the job offered, even if it's not an ideal fit.

Sometimes a job is just a job! We do it to earn money. Not EVERYBODY can live their dreams! If they did, the bathrooms would NEVER get cleaned because... NOBODY dreams of cleaning toilets! ~Scotty Gunther

Trial and error is the only real way of figuring out what your personal communication style is. It's called learning through experience. You will make mistakes but remember, if you say something that gets you fired, then you will know not to say that again. This might seem a bit extreme, but I AM comfortable communicating through this style. (Which is the whole point of tip number eight!)

Tip: 9

Put down your stupid smart phone!

In this world of always being connected, we are becoming totally disconnected. Too many people rely on electronic devices to communicate.

Put away your smart phone or Blackberry and refrain from text messaging, or Facebooking as refreshing ways to return to face-to-face interaction.

I wonder if there is way to unfriend MYSELF on facebook? ~Scotty Gunther

Make it a point to have a personal conversation with someone in your office every day.

It's NOT facebook stalking...if they don't know you are doing it! ~Scotty Gunther

It's easy to see that too many people rely on electronic devices to communicate in the workplace. Stand out by talking with people in person. Like any skill, if you don't use them you lose them. There is no faster way to become business socially awkward than to always have your face buried in your stupid phone!

Now, I understand that social networking is the big buzz, and while these things can help you find customers and get new business, your ability to communicate properly to them, is the only way that will keep your customers happy! So put down the Ipad and say...HELLO!

Tip: 10

Become a better listener.

The key to becoming a better communicator is to become a better listener. Which means, simply Listen, more than you talk. Obviously, I DO HAVE A PROBLEM WITH THIS!!!

Listening shows that you are confident enough to know that you don't always have to be the one talking. It's important to be confident and be positive. I have never met a successful person who isn't a good listener and who isn't an optimist.

I am only going to focus on the positive from now on! No more worrying about the crazy, loser, negative morons, who....awww shoot, Well, so much for that! ~Scotty Gunther

Conclusion

Always remember that, communication is an important part of any work or life situation. It can make your time at work a lot more enjoyable.

Now it's time to put these lessons into practice. But before we do, let's recap. We have learned that,

"Communicating way more better" means:

- Communicate loud enough so others can hear you.

- Speak the other person's language.

- Always be aware of nonverbal communication.

- Be less serious.

- Appear to be open and honest.

- Avoid mimicking or mirroring others.

- Care about your customers and co-workers.

- Be comfortable communicating in your own style.

- Use your smart phone or mobile devices a little less.

- Be a better listener.

About The Author

Scotty Gunther's 25-year overnight success story is an ongoing journey. Born in Michigan, Scotty Gunther is a comedian, author, speaker, emcee, and award-winning syndicated radio host. His unique combination of original voice, ability to connect, improvisation, innovation, and an authentic "all or nothing" view on business, communications, creativity, relationships and life has captured the attention of audiences throughout the U.S. and Canada.

On the radio, Scotty Gunther is hilarious yet insightful and can be heard giving relationship advice to women, and some sensitive men...all two of them. Scotty had the highest (age 18-34) rated top-40 afternoon show in the country before leaving to launch, "Scotty Says," a nationally syndicated relationship based comedy and advice feature heard on radio stations across the country.

Scotty Gunther is the logical voice of reason in this dizzying and insane world of business, communications, creativity and relationships. His advice has been featured in national self-help magazines and newspapers throughout the US. Scotty has given advice and tips directly impacting celebrities, professional athletes, reality television stars, and multi-platinum recording artists.

On stage, Scotty Gunther has performed at more than 2,000 colleges, corporations, comedy clubs, conferences, and private shows. He was recently named the top emcee in North America for 2008, 2009, 2010, and 2011. Scotty can be seen performing his highly sought after shows and programs, *The Couples' Challenge*, *The Co-workers' Challenge* and *The Singles' Challenge*. These shows are a mix of comedy and crowd participation. You'll find more booking and show information available at:

www.scottysays.com
www.thecoupleschallenge.com
www.coworkerschallenge.com
www.thesingleschallenge.com

Lectures, Motivation, Team Building and Comedy Entertainment

Scotty Gunther is also available for his "communicate way more better" lecture, motivational team building, and comedy entertainment events anywhere in the world.

Business and Corporate events: Scotty Gunther's *Co-workers' Challenge,* is a unique team building activity, great for bringing life to your next staff or corporate event. The focus is very much about fun, interaction and laughter.

This team building activities consist of two-person co-worker teams and five rounds. Each round has lively questions and engaging team activity. This show helps to strengthen team spirit as participants learn more about their co-workers. There is no better way to create playful camaraderie and build a successful team atmosphere. Laughter relaxes and connects people, while creating a strong bond. Mixed with positive messages about communication and motivation, *The Co-Workers Challenge* is the perfect team building activity.

"Communicate way more better!" live is also available for business events.

www.coworkerschallenge.com

Comedy: Looking for a show that really connects with everyone? Scotty Gunther's The *Couples' Challenge* show is part stand-up comedy, and part crowd participation. Scotty uses humor to defuse the serious nature of life's issues and his relationship comedy is directly relevant to everyone's life. Scotty will test your relationship when we find out how well you know your mate. This show is great for conferences, festivals, colleges, nightclubs, restaurants, casinos, concerts, comedy clubs, or any event.

www.theCoupleschallenge.com

Dating or singles events: Make your singles or dating event unforgettable by having Relationship Realist, Scotty Gunther host and perform his *Singles' Challenge* show about accountability in dating and relationships that will fill the room with laughter. The perfect icebreaker, Scotty will ease tension with his unique, quick, honest, "all-or-nothing" relationship based humor and advice that will directly connect with your guests. Scotty's authentic approach to dating will help make your event special and unforgettable.

www.Thesingleschallenge.com

Host and emcee

Do you have an event? Hire the 2008, 2009,2010, and 2011 top emcee in North America, Scotty Gunther as the master of ceremonies (MC/emcee) for your next special event. Sure, you could get an amateur to perform the duties. But it's much better to have a seasoned professional engage the audience, make announcements, thank the sponsors, present awards, and keep everyone entertained.

If you want entertainment at your event, hire a professional Master of Ceremonies. An experienced emcee will handle:

- Introducing the acts throughout the event

- Entertaining the crowd with unique, humorous content and filling in time between acts as needed

- Thanking the sponsors and making announcements

- Plugging event merchandise

- Acting as a point-of-contact for questions.

Available on audio CD at Amazon.com createspace.com Amazon mp3 and Scottysays.com

Scotty Gunther's, *Jerk-B-Gone*.

Jerk-B-Gone is for women who are sick and tired of attracting the wrong type of guys. *Jerk-B-Gone* is a unique mix of relationship comedy, motivation, and real life tools and tips that will help you get rid of the jerks in your life! If you are convinced that you are a jerk-magnet, this hilarious but insightful CD program will help you remove the losers, liars, creeps and cheaters while teaching you how to attract the love that you have always wanted. And you will do this while laughing along the way.

Pete's Papaya.

Pete's Papaya by Scotty Gunther is a modern day parable about motivation, bravery, diversity and business.

"The small farm town of Appleton has always been the place to go to get fresh apples. Until the day a man named Pete shows up with an odd-looking fruit and dares to sell something besides apples in Appleton."

For more Scotty Gunther books, products or information on Scotty's comedy shows, advice and live entertainment. Visit: **www.scottysays.com**